BRIDAL
FLOWERS

BRIDAL
Flowers

Arrangements for a Perfect Wedding

MARIA MCBRIDE-MELLINGER

photography by

WILLIAM STITES

A Bulfinch Press Book

Little, Brown and Company   Boston o Toronto o London

Dedication TO MY HUSBAND BRETT, MY BEST FRIEND

Produced by Smallwood and Stewart, Inc., New York City
Design: Dirk Kaufman
Flowers on half-title page: Blue Meadow Flowers
Flowers on title page verso: Curtis M. Godwin

First Edition
ISBN 0-8212-1917-0

Library of Congress Catalog Card Number 91-58122

Library of Congress Cataloging-in-Publication information
is available.

Bulfinch Press is an imprint and trademark of Little, Brown
and Company (Inc.).
Published simultaneously in Canada by Little, Brown &
Company (Canada) Limited

PRINTED IN SINGAPORE

Tokens of

Affection

For centuries, brides have carried bouquets and wedding sites have been decorated with flowers. Beyond the standard floral choices for today's bride—a nosegay of white roses or a cascade of baby's breath, carnations, and ivy— there are countless exciting possibilities, and choosing wedding flowers can be an opportunity to set a distinctive personal tone for your wedding. The pages that follow show that there are also many other uses for flowers besides the bouquet: You can transform an en-

trance with an arch of blooming forsythia branches; trim gifts with delicate silk primroses; combine tiny grape hyacinths with full-blown peonies for dramatic centerpieces; gild petals, leaves, and stems to create a dazzling twist to nature. Or recreate the traditional bouquet with unexpected floral combinations—by filling the centers of four or five large white 'Casablanca' lilies with miniature red rosebuds, for example, and finishing the nosegay with a collar of larger red roses.

Today there are no strict rules for wedding flowers; instead there are many flexible guidelines to help you design your arrangements. The starting principle is to know yourself. You will be the focal point on this important day, and you will be most at ease if you match the

style of your wedding to your personality. Ideally, the overall effect should be a blend of compatible details: The style and color of the bride's bouquet should set the tone for all the other flowers at the ceremony and reception—even the groom's boutonniere—and should be in harmony with your dress. Every element of the wedding should lend a sense of unity to the occasion, and—most importantly—should complement rather than outshine the tenderness of the moment.

CHOOSING A FLORAL DESIGNER

You should begin your search for a floral designer at least three months in advance of the wedding date. If the designer is particularly

Reception arrangements can be simple: Bind together two dozen French tulips, preceding page, and plant them in an interesting cachepot (VSF). A simple tulle skirt can be studded with fresh flowers such as these American roses finished with gilded ivy leaves, left (Bobby Wiggins). A pomander of American 'Bridal White' and 'Bridal Pink' roses, above, is a charming and practical option for children to carry (Carolien Stikker).

*The right headpiece works well with fresh flowers, above, and generally
a clean, simple design is the best balance for eye-catching blooms. Pin the flowers
directly into your hair after your headpiece is in place (Curtis M. Godwin). Delicate and
fresh, an all-white cascade of individually wired Dutch sweet peas, right, is a
graceful choice (Bobby Wiggins).*

popular, however, you may need to reserve him or her as much as a year in advance. Equally, if your wedding date falls at the height of the wedding season between May and August, or on a busy flower-giving day such as Mother's Day, Valentine's Day, or any major holiday, you should reserve your floral designer as early as possible.

Begin your search by asking friends and relatives for recommendations. You may have attended a party or even another wedding in the recent past where the flowers were particularly memorable. Ask the host or hostess for the floral designer's name and find out what it was like working with him or her. You may have seen photographs of flowers you like. In magazines the florist's name and location will generally be given; if not, contact the magazine for information. If you can't get a reference from someone you know, put together a list of designers in your area using the local yellow pages, and visit each one. Ask banquet managers and ministers to recommend floral designers who have decorated weddings and other special events held at their locations.

A floral designer should be someone you can trust, not simply to manage the flowers but to bring energy and creative talents to the event itself. Most will be connected with a retail shop, which you should visit to get a feeling for the designer's style and taste. His or her primary responsibility, however, may be to the store and you may not get the personal attention you want—especially if it is a large business since many larger firms take on more than one wedding a day. If personal attention is a priority, you may prefer to hire a designer with a small shop or private business.

When judging a retail designer, evaluate the shop. A creative, versatile designer will have a beautifully decorated store with eye-catching window displays. Avoid stores that look dated and unkempt, have old or unhealthy flowers in the refrigerator, or feature only a few standard types of blooms. If the designer only works privately, it's important to see samples of his or her work. Ask to visit an event in progress or to see photographs from a recent affair. You could even order an arrangement to evaluate. Are the

*Hand-calligraphy will personalize a ceremony announcement, left,
trimmed with smilax, stephanotis, and roses (Bobby Wiggins). Flowers should
highlight the architecturally interesting spots at your reception—this mantel, above, blooms
with flowering plum branches, Dutch 'Star Gazer' and 'Casablanca' lilies,
ranunculus, roses, and grape hyacinths (Curtis M. Godwin).*

Trimmings of silk primroses and roses transform a wedding gift, above,
into something very special (Dulken & Derrick, gift wrapping by Anne-Stuart
Hamilton). A special going-away bouquet, right, like this one of grape hyacinths in a collar
of Serena roses and blush-pink roses, can be tossed or kept (Curtis M. Godwin).

flowers fresh? If you made specific requests, were they followed; if not, did the florist provide appropriate substitutions? Is the mix between flowers and foliage balanced? Most importantly, do you like it?

Ask how much of a designer's business is devoted to weddings. If it's sizeable, you'll feel more secure knowing the florist can handle any problem or request that may surface. Many floral designers can act as party planners. Not only can they design the flowers for your event, but they can also rent a wide assortment of items—from furniture and fabrics to ornamental columns—to spruce up or personalize any reception location.

Once you find a retail or private designer with a style that appeals to you, ask for references. Find out if previous clients were happy with the designer's attentiveness and professionalism. Finally, decide if you are comfortable talking to the designer about how you envision your event. If you feel intimidated by his or her attitude, go elsewhere. It's imper-

ative you hire someone who is both talented and responsive to your suggestions and desires.

During your first appointment with the floral designer you hire, be prepared to discuss the details of your dress, the size and style of your wedding party, the location of the ceremony and reception, your ideas for the flowers, and the budget you have in mind. A good designer will visit the wedding and reception locations, evaluate fabric swatches, view Polaroids of the wedding party dresses, and incorporate your ideas into the overall design scheme. By your second meeting, the designer should be prepared to present suggestions and offer price estimates.

Although the wedding day is the focus of this book, there are many other events during the engagement period that call for floral decorations. The ideas in the pages that follow can easily be adapted for engagement parties, bridal showers, or to create thank-you gifts for mothers enabling you to refine your relationship with your florist.

idal Party

Whether you have a dozen maids and ushers standing up for you or only one, the bridal party will take its floral cues from the bride and groom. Flower girls, bridesmaids, and the maid of honor attend the bride and all usually carry or wear flowers. The groom, his father, the ushers, and the bride's father or escort generally wear boutonnieres. Although mothers and grandmothers of the bride and groom are considered members of the bridal party, flowers for them are optional.

The earliest weddings were more than just joyous events. They were communal celebrations, hallmarks of change and continuity, rituals of passage that would ensure the viability of the culture. Such a momentous day called for gala festivities, trimmed with all the flowers and fruits available to the community.

Engraved Athenian wedding urns dating from the sixth century B.C. depict details of the nuptial ceremony, which included herbal flourishes for the bridal couple and garlanded bridal chambers. Herbs were carefully chosen for adornment. Plants like mint and marigold, noted for their aphrodisiac qualities, were used in garlands and wreaths, as were sesame and poppy, which symbolized fertility. Other cultures used pungent herbs like garlic to ward off evil spirits and guarantee a happy and prosperous start for the newlyweds. A tradition of tossing grains of wheat at the bride to symbolize fruitfulness emerged in Rome during the first century B.C.

Gradually, the traditional usage of flowers and herbs in wedding ceremonies was broadened to include not only those plants attributed with certain qualities, like aphrodisiacs, but also those that symbolized feelings, such as roses for love. In Elizabethan England, friends of the bride would give the groom a nosegay of rosemary, symbolizing faithfulness, to ensure the bride's happiness.

Although elements of the ceremony and bridal costume date back to the early days of civilization, most of the traditions we now follow originated in the Victorian era. The Victorians codified the elaborate language of flowers we know today. Friends and lovers communicated secret messages with the flowers they

Update the traditional all-white nosegay with unusual combinations,
preceding page, such as creamy roses mixed with fresh wheat and kale leaves wired together
to create true "cabbage roses" (Bobby Wiggins). An armful of white calla lilies, left, is
always a dramatic choice. French braid a ribbon over the stems for an elegant finish
(Curtis M. Godwin). A mix of spring flowers crafted from silk, above, is a keepsake
that will last forever (Dulken & Derrick, design Bobby Wiggins).

These unusual miniature Dutch salmon-pink calla lilies give a formal edge to
this country nosegay, above, of white lilacs and viburnum (Bobby Wiggins). Dozens of
separate white gladioli blooms were wired together to create a camellia-like
flower known as a "glamellia," right. Gilded silk ivy finishes
the bouquet (Curtis M. Godwin).

exchanged. Not only did individual blooms have special significance—such as bachelor's button for hope, hyacinth for constancy, and lily for purity—but the color of the bloom itself added yet another layer of innuendo. Roses, for example, have always meant love, but while in the language of flowers a

red rose says "I love you," a yellow rose signifies love on the wane. The specific arrangement of a nosegay would likewise create a code: The first initial of each flower could be used to spell messages or names. Victorians also replaced the wreath brides traditionally wore in their hair with sprigs of orange blossom and a bridal veil to symbolize virginal purity. Another popular Victorian tradition was to plant a sprig—usually myrtle, representing love—from the bridal bouquet after the wedding.

BOUQUET TRADITIONS

Flowers have a timeless elegance and grace and a natural delicacy that makes them the acces-

sory of choice for every bride. A bridal adornment since antiquity, the bouquet has nevertheless changed dramatically in shape and style over the ages.

Early in this century, brides lugged massive shower bouquets down the aisle. Often up to two feet in diameter, these lavish arrangements made of gardenias, lilies, and roses were trimmed with greenery such as ferns and herbs, and with ribbons and love knots. With the changing economy and the streamlined fashions of the 1920s and 30s, the bridal bouquet shrank to a manageable posy. Simple in construction, these nosegays most often featured lilies of the valley, gardenias, camellias, or orange blossoms. Trimming the bridal gown with flowers—most often fresh orange blossoms at the waist—was a popular alternative to the bouquet. Garlands of lilies of the valley, nasturtiums, and pansies were spirited options for the lively, looser flapper designs.

During the 1940s, wartime rationing crippled the bridal market. Farmers replaced non-

The gentle pastel tones of sweet peas, roses, winter jasmine, Dusty
Miller, and Queen Anne's lace, left, create a demure feeling (Lawrence Becker).
By contrast, combining vivid colors achieves a dramatic look such as this spirited mix of
Dutch calla lilies and 'Art Shade' cattleya orchids, above (Bobby Wiggins).

*After white, pink is the most popular bridal color—but it doesn't have
to be the traditional sweet, soft pink. Mix candy-striped tulips with dianthus for
a fresh look, top. Red and white are a classic choice for a holiday bouquet, bottom. Here
the opulence of deep ruby-red roses is set against creamy ruffled
kale leaves (both Bobby Wiggins).*

*The variegated form of Dutch dianthus, top, highlights their ruffled
edges for an informal yet lively nosegay for any season (VSF). Vibrant electric-
yellow calla lilies, brilliant orange-and-red striped parrot tulips, and orange ranunculus,
contrasted with fluffy creamy-green viburnum are a vivid yet harmonious
blend in this dramatic design, bottom (Bobby Wiggins).*

*Larger blooms are often most graceful as an arm bouquet resting on
your forearm. Combine colors in the same family, such as these pink peonies,
Dutch 'Nicole' roses, and purple lilacs, above. Creating a composite flower is a technique
from the past: Single 'Casablanca' lily petals are wired around lilies of the
valley, right, and the stems wrapped with antique velvet ribbon
(both Alexandra Randall).*

vital crops like flowers with food crops to aid the war effort, and fresh flowers became virtually impossible to obtain. Fabric flowers became the patriotic choice for the wartime bride.

After the war, farmers returned to cultivating flowers. The rebirth and growth of the floraculture market and the eager consumerism of the 1950s triggered a brief flirtation with large bouquets reminiscent of the earlier shower bouquets. By the end of the decade, however, controlled nosegays won out as the best design for the explosive "new look" in fashion, characterized by tailored waists and full, shorter skirts. By the end of the radical 1960s the "politically correct" bouquet called for simple, hand-tied flowers such as daffodils and primroses. Many brides carried a few daisies as the peaceful, "mod" alternative of the hippie generation.

The earthy 1970s witnessed a return to bouquets composed of masses of garden blooms, primarily flowering herbs and wildflowers like heather, aster, and Queen Anne's lace. These deliberately undesigned armloads or basketsful of flowers had a natural, picked-fresh-from-the-garden quality.

The opulent 1980s sanctioned personal indulgence and encouraged dramatic displays of wealth. These expensive, hard-to-hold, labor-intensive bouquets widely copied Lady Diana's wedding flowers of cascading stephanotis, roses, variegated ivy, and phalaenopsis orchids. Ecology and economics are hallmarks of the practical 1990s, and mark a return to well-crafted, manageable bouquets. Yet today's wide range of bridal fashion, from satin ball gowns to lacy minidresses, opens the door to a greater array of floral options than ever before, including freeze-dried flowers, evergreens, unusual fresh flowers, and exquisite hand-made silk flowers.

YOUR BRIDAL BOUQUET

In spirit the modern bouquet borrows the best of the past; its design relies on the talents of an experienced floral designer and spotlights the imagination of the bride.

The key to selecting flowers for your wedding ensemble is to remember that they are only accessories. Like your jewelry and shoes, flowers should complement, and never upstage your look. You are not a vehicle for transporting a floral arrangement down the aisle. The overall effect should be beautiful, gentle, and balanced. Don't agree to a floral design that feels heavy—it will only make you appear awkward. A bouquet whose proper handling requires concentration is not appropriate for the wedding day when there will be so many other things to think about. The ideal bouquet should rest comfortably and easily in your arms.

Coordinating the flowers that you want with the dress that you have selected is easier than you might think. Proportion is the key to achieving the right balance: The bigger the dress, the bigger the bouquet. The same holds true for the size of the bride. A statuesque bride can carry a larger bouquet; petite brides look best holding smaller nosegays.

Formal and traditional weddings require a different kind of bouquet than one for informal and contemporary weddings. Most formal weddings take place in a grand location with lots of attendants and many guests. The bridal gown for such an affair usually features a long

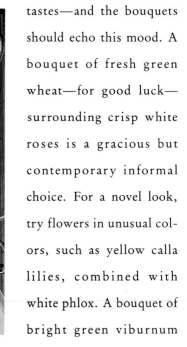

train and a very full skirt. In keeping with the mood of the occasion, many formal wedding bouquets use no more than a few types of flowers. A mass of all-white lilies of the valley, roses, or stephanotis is a timeless and elegant choice.

Informal bouquet options are endless. While formal affairs aim for classic elegance, informal weddings cleverly mix personal attitudes and tastes—and the bouquets should echo this mood. A bouquet of fresh green wheat—for good luck—surrounding crisp white roses is a gracious but contemporary informal choice. For a novel look, try flowers in unusual colors, such as yellow calla lilies, combined with white phlox. A bouquet of bright green viburnum edged with fresh green maple leaves will complement the most unconventional dress.

Regardless of the size or tone of the wedding, brides have traditionally opted for all-white bouquets. White has long been the color associated with all things bridal. Brides began wearing white for their weddings as early as the sixteenth century. Then, white was a reflection of familial wealth, rather than a symbol of

The best silk flowers have to be touched to tell them apart from fresh.
Because they are more durable, they are a practical choice for adorning bridal
veils, left, and gowns (Dulken & Derrick, La Sposa veil). Highlight the lines of a simple
gown, above, with a long boa of astilbe, American 'Bridal White' and Dutch
'Porcelana' roses (Leslie Kyle Ferrar).

Ordinary baby's breath, above, is spectacular when carried alone.
Counterbalance its mass by dotting your hair with individual blooms (Bobby
Wiggins). An antique basket, right, showcases a medley of country garden favorites: lilacs,
columbines, hyacinths, dianthus, campanulas, larkspur, eucharyis lilies, and
bleeding hearts (Curtis M. Godwin).

Affordable fresh flower bounty can be limited in winter. Rely instead on seasonal foliage to broaden your design options, like a sheath of mixed evergreens with gilded pinecones, Dutch stephanotis, and dianthus, above (Bobby Wiggins) or a simple bright-red berry bouquet, right (Flowers Forever).

virginity—the bride's virtue was always assumed. Only the well-to-do could afford to dress in a color so easily soiled and made specifically for just one day. Much later, the Victorians firmly established the tradition of a white wedding gown as a reflection of joy. White flowers were a natural accompaniment, although not used exclusively.

Today, popular white bridal flowers include gardenias, calla lilies, lilies of the valley, roses, orchids, stephanotis, hydrangeas, tulips, lilacs, peonies, freesias, irises, and madonna lilies. For a truly dramatic formal bouquet, carry a cluster of calla lilies, or a nosegay of lisianthus and eucharis lilies. But working with a floral designer opens up many other alternatives to the conventional bouquet, such as making a single large composite flower from the individual petals of many larger flowers, like lilies or gladiola, finished and held with a single gilded stem.

Perhaps the most versatile bouquet shape is the nosegay—a round design, usually six to eight inches in diameter, anchored in a bouquet holder or hand-tied—because it is easy to carry and adaptable for most flowers. From tight designs composed of tiny violets, miniature roses, and bachelor's buttons to larger, looser bundles of full-blown blooms such as old-fashioned roses or double tulips, nosegays offer endless options for creating a striking effect with almost any flower. You can create a very dramatic bouquet with a riot of orchids, a gentle pastel palette with garden roses, or a fresh, seasonal touch with a knot of spring flowers like grape hyacinths and double narcissus. Concentric rings of colorful tiny pansies and forget-me-nots make a very sweet and simple nosegay, known as a Biedermeier; a mass of baby's breath will look light and informal; and a fragrant nosegay of verdant herbs like heather and sea grass has a fresh, country feeling.

Although the nosegay is the most functional shape, some flowers look best in an arm-held design. Hand-tied arm bouquets, a linear de-

sign in which the blooms are nestled at your elbow and the stems along your forearm, celebrate the graceful lines of long-stemmed flowers like calla lilies, French tulips, or peonies. You can carry a sheaf of pine, a harvest of lilac and peonies, or a mix of summer wildflowers. For unusual floral combinations, many floral designers hand-wire tender or short-stemmed blossoms like sweet peas and violets to blend them into bouquets with larger and heartier hand-tied flowers. Cascading designs use a mix of these techniques. Cascades work best with small light flowers: A cascading mass of large roses will look (and sometimes be) heavy. Opt instead for shorter, lighter cascades of dendrobium orchids, or a mass of tiny blooms like delphiniums or euphorbia. But a good bouquet need not be complex. Some flowers work well alone: three or four graphic blooms of phalaenopsis orchids, for example, or a single larger flower like hydrangea.

Manipulating nature is part of the excitement of floral artistry. However, floral designers should not torture flowers into stiff or overly structured shapes. Your designer may remove excess petals from massive blooms to make smaller, more compact arrangements, or add more petals to a small bud to create a composite flower, or eliminate distracting foliage and pare away multiple stems from the final bouquet without fighting the natural grace of the flower.

Scent can be an important consideration when you are selecting flowers for your bouquet. If you design around your favorite scented bloom, be it lavender or old-fashioned roses, then that fragrance will forever evoke fond memories of your wedding. But although everyone naturally identifies flowers with a sensuous aroma, many of the most popular commercially grown flowers sadly have little or no scent. The glorious hybrid blooms we treasure for visual appeal have been cultivated for color, size, shape, and longevity and often their precious scent has been lost in the process. Still, you can find beautiful flowers noted for their scent: Gardenias, lilies of the valley, hyacinths, violets, lilacs, lavender, sweet peas, freesias, some peonies, and old-fashioned roses all emit a luscious fragrance.

A reproduction of a Victorian posy holder, left, contains tiny pansies
and grape hyacinths. Above, a gilded bouquet base holds a Biedermeier:
Concentric rings of tightly packed blooms including Dutch nerines, Serena and 'Pink
Delight' roses, grape hyacinths, lilies of the valley, and dianthus. Antique silk
leaves finish the bouquet (both Bobby Wiggins).

The traditional finishing touch on most bouquets is a ribbon and bow. Satin-faced, velvet, or wired ribbons enrich any bouquet. Arm-held bouquets with longer, exposed stems are a more formal look when a narrow ribbon is braided over the stems. Not only is it more beautiful but it is also more delicate against your hands. If your floral designer does not stock a wide assortment of ribbons, you can choose among the variety of unusual, beautiful ribbons available at many specialty stores.

Don't overlook the wide variety of alternatives to a bouquet as you consider your options. Keep your mind open to your designer's suggestions—they will know what is in season or affordable and even what flowers are newly available—and look beyond your immediate personal favorites when you consider which flowers to choose for the wedding. Ask the designer to show you reference material so you can review photographs of available flowers. The Flower Council of Holland distributes two useful tools: "The Cut Flower Booklet" features over six hundred popular and unusual flower varieties, and "The Color Chart", which keys Dutch flowers to hundreds of color shades that can be matched to any fabric swatch. Most florists carry these or you can order them by mail (see Resources).

Designers typically make the bouquets and arrangements the day of the wedding. Most flowers, properly conditioned, will easily last through the ceremony and reception. If you are to be married on the hottest day of the year, your floral designer will recommend the hardier blooms that will be readily available. If your designer will not be present for the start of the ceremony, make sure you receive detailed instructions for handling the flowers. Although commercially-sold flowers have been conditioned before you receive them to prolong their life, if they arrive some time before the ceremony it is important keep them under the optimum conditions.

There are many things you and your floral designer can do to keep your flowers looking fresh. Once bouquets are delivered they should be handled as little as possible until the cere-

The bride's veil is an age-old symbol of purity and maidenhood. Glue tender sweet pea blossoms, "delicate pleasures" in the language of flowers, over the veil, left, and blend the traditions of the past with your own (Leslie Kyle Ferrar).

Brides from the 1920s trimmed their gowns with fresh flowers, usually orange blossoms.
Any hardy flower with a soft stem should pin easily to your gown. Try Dutch astilbe and
roses, above, to highlight a dramatic neckline (Leslie Kyle Ferrar).

*If you want the look of fresh flowers but don't want to worry about
their perishability, consider a bridal gown trimmed with silk flowers, such
as the Carolina Herrera gown, above left, or the one from Loris Azzaro,
Paris, above right (Vera Wang Bridal House Ltd.).*

mony. If your bouquet is hand-tied, with exposed stems, keep the flowers in fresh cold water until the last possible moment. Nosegays anchored in a bouquet holder have an oasis saturated with water and will be long-lasting. Bouquets as well as boutonnieres should arrive well-misted and packaged in cellophane to maximize their life span. On exceptionally hot days, keep a large cooler on hand and leave your flowers in it until you're ready to walk down the aisle. In winter, freezing temperatures can be equally hard on delicate petals. Keep the flowers away from the cold and drafts as well as from heating ducts and radiators; any temperature extreme will be damaging to the flowers.

OTHER FLORAL OPTIONS

Hand-crafted flowers are an option to fresh flowers for the bouquet and generally require less special handling. Properly executed, they can be every bit as exquisite as the real thing and, of course, are not dependent on season. Fabric designers have reproduced every living flower in more colors than are found in nature. Silk lends itself well to a wide range of bouquets: Lined with wire, it is supple enough to be shaped into any design. Alternatively, traditional dried flowers and newly available freeze-dried flowers capture delicate blooms forever, though dried flowers can be extremely fragile. Because of their delicacy and shorter stems, dried designs work best when held firmly in nosegays or hand-tied bouquets. The most durable of hand-crafted flowers are those made from glass beads. A sophisticated alternative to a corsage, these flowers make beautiful keepsakes for the mothers of the newlyweds.

Most floral designers can provide silk or

Adorn yourself with blossoms from your head to your toe, above.
Petite fresh Serena roses and silk bachelor buttons—something blue—
trim this bridal shoe (Curtis M. Godwin). A floral wreath looks lavish but is easy
to wear when crafted from small flowers, right: Stephanotis, white roses,
Dusty Miller, and hyacinths (Lawrence Becker).

*The ancients would adorn brides with blooms, a beautiful tradition
that can be updated in so many ways. Fill a wide-brimmed hat, above, with a
potpourri of Dutch flowers—roses, calla lilies, tulips, poppies, ranunculus, viburnum,
and grape hyacinths. A necklace of roses, daffodils, scabiosa, and other flowers
wired together and tied to a ribbon, right, is more beautiful
than pearls (both Bobby Wiggins).*

dried flowers. However, many specialty stores and catalogs supply these and other flowers. They can be ordered to arrive weeks before the ceremony, giving you plenty of time to alter the arrangement or to add your own personal touches.

Baskets, easy to carry and available in many sizes, colors, and textures, are a natural vessel for wedding flowers. Wildflowers like cornflowers, foxgloves, daisies, and thistles look best in rough country baskets; prim Victorian baskets are better for delicate blooms like anemones, lupines, and primroses.

The bouquet is not the only floral option for the bride. Flowers make memorable accessories during and especially after the ceremony. Wear a hat brimming over with lilacs, spray roses, or tulips, or a floral necklace of scabiosa, freesia, and eustoma. Trim your train with a vine of gilded ivy: Let your imagination take flight.

THE BEST MAN AND USHERS

Whether the attire of choice is a suit or formal wear, the groom and his men, including his father and yours, will each wear a boutonniere. The boutonnieres should be the same, but the groom's can have a distinctive look, though it should never be larger than the others. If the other men wear white rose boutonnieres, the groom can wear a red rose, for example. Custom suggests the groom wear a flower from the bridal bouquet on his lapel: If the bridal bouquet is not composed of large blooms, have the groom wear one of the same flowers. At the least, the men's boutonnieres should complement the flowers worn by the bride and her attendants. Many ceremonies include a moment when the bride "plucks" a prepared boutonniere from her bouquet and pins it to her groom's lapel, but most nervous couples find this procedure a little too tricky.

Boutonnieres should be restrained. Anything larger than a medium-size rose is too big. The length should be no more than about four inches, including the stem. A single bloom like a rose or carnation is most common, but an asymmetrical design works very well. Combine three small stephanotis buds or, at the most, five miniature blooms like Serena roses

Boutonnieres are best constructed from buds and miniature flowers.
A single bud is always classic, but the alternatives are endless. Serena roses
and grape hyacinths, left, are a fresh springtime option (Curtis M. Godwin). Gild a
rose leaf and use it to back stephanotis and a sprig of white lilac,
above, for a holiday wedding (Bobby Wiggins).

*Petals are useful in many ways. A boutonniere, above, of three
white Serena roses is backed by a single red-rose petal instead of greenery (Bobby
Wiggins). Rose petals—to scatter before the bride—fill a wicker basket, right, trimmed
with azaela, roses, and wax flowers (Blue Meadow Flowers).*

for the right balance. Don't forget to include a small leaf such as ivy to finish the boutonniere. Freesia set against a dark green galyx leaf is a fragrant alternative. If the men prefer to wear handkerchiefs in their dinner jackets or suits, eliminate the boutonnieres.

THE BRIDE'S ATTENDANTS

The bride must have at least one attendant at her wedding ceremony but she may choose as many more as she wishes. Attendants traditionally include bridesmaids and flower girls; however, little boys are welcome additions in the bridal procession and children can attend the bride in lieu of bridesmaids.

Many brides have at least five bridesmaids; one has special status as the maid (or matron) of honor. Her responsibilities generally include coordinating the gowns and accessories of the bridal party and hosting a bridal shower. On the day of the wedding, the maid of honor helps the bride dress, makes sure the rest of the party is properly attired, arranges the bride's train and veil at the ceremony, and holds her bouquet during the exchange of vows. In recognition of her special status, the maid of honor usually carries a distinctive bouquet. Although similar to the other bouquets in size and color, her bouquet will often have a special touch. If the bridesmaids carry nosegays of white carnations, for example, the maid of honor might carry the same nosegay embellished with a collar of white stocks.

Bridesmaids' bouquets should echo the color and shape of the larger bridal bouquet. If the bride carries a nosegay, her attendants should, too. The tones of the bridesmaids' flowers should complement not only their own dresses, but also the bridal bouquet. Their bouquets need not be identical, although this is a beautiful, simple option. Variously hued bouquets in the same color family offer a refreshing switch from a monochromatic scheme. However, a crisp alternative is for everyone in the bridal party to carry white flowers.

Bridesmaids can also wear flowers. Although flower-trimmed hats can be attractive, it is hard to find a hat style that looks flattering on everyone; loose flowers in the hair may be

*Children are a delight to have at any wedding. Trim a silk headband
with pansies and lilies of the valley, above left, or fill a miniature watering can,
above right, with pansies, miniature pink calla lilies, ixia, and lilies of the valley
(both Curtis M. Godwin).*

*A ring pillow, above left, made from moss and decorated
with galyx leaves, variegated ivy, pansies, hyacinths, stephanotis,
and a basket, above right, of roses, lilacs, calla lilies, and stephanotis are manageable
treats for little hands (both Bobby Wiggins).*

Consider wearing any one of the many floral-inspired accessories
available, above—gloves, earrings, a silk flowered handbag, and a crystal posy.
Posies spun from sugar are a charming option for children to carry; mothers treasure these
small confections instead of a corsage, right (Gail Watson).

easier to use. Even if the bride wears a hat, it is not necessary for the bridesmaids to follow her lead. It is more appealing to trim a bridesmaid's hair with flowers than to rely on a prepared, hard-to-wear headpiece. If possible, have the women wear their hair up, then add a comb of flowers at the nape of the neck. Small

flowers like sweet william work best because they are lightweight and anchor easily in place. Or fashion a headband by pinning small clusters of baby's breath in place with bobby pins.

A procession of children bearing flowers adds charm to every wedding ceremony. There is no need to limit the number of children, especially if you have more than one important child in your life. To create a special moment at the beginning of the ceremony, have the children carry a garland down the aisle and lay it on the altar as a decoration. Or give them small bouquets to carry to mothers and grandmothers of the bride and groom once they are seated.

The children's flowers should be easy for small hands to hold—a heavy or awkward bouquet will cause trouble—and use the same color scheme as the adults in the bridal party. Small posies of freesias, ixia, and mini-gladioli, or violets or pansies alone, a pomander of rosebuds, a garland of smilax trimmed with dendrobium orchids for several children to share, or baskets of petals are all lovely options. Not only will the party look more uniform, but the children will find less opportunity for dissension if they all carry the same or very similar designs.

Mothers and grandmothers of the bride and groom have traditionally worn corsages. Corsages tend to look fussy and old-fashioned, however, and this custom is declining also because the fine fabrics of their dresses won't support the weight of a corsage. But don't break their hearts if they really want to wear flowers. Opt for a small cluster of flowers or a single camellia. Alternatively, let them carry small posies presented to them by the children before the ceremony.

The

Ceremony

No matter what kind of ceremony you choose—civil or religious, formal or informal, brief or long—decorating the wedding site with flowers underscores the dignity and grace of the occasion, adds a sense of celebration and joy, and symbolizes the timeless promise of the union. In England during the Middle Ages, weddings were typically large, festive events open to all. Members of the parish would escort the bride and groom through town to church, petals were often strewn in

the bride's path to guarantee happiness, and the event would be celebrated at the church door. But in the eighteenth-century, a tax levied on public weddings brought an end to these bois- terous, communal celebrations.

Today, the majority of marriages still take place in a house of worship; but the ser- vice itself is often held at a different location than the reception. If you plan to use different locations for the service and the reception, you should follow a few simple guidelines:

◦ Choose locations accessible to each other. You may want to have your wedding at a charm- ing country chapel, but this is not practical if the nearest reception area is forty-five min- utes away.

◦ Both locations should have plenty of park-

ing. If not, or if the lo- cation is hard to find, you should consider hiring transportation for guests.

◦ Decorations for the wedding space should be installed at least an hour before the ser- vice. Guests, espe- cially those unfamiliar with the area, tend to arrive early and should not witness the prepa- rations. Ask the rector

or rabbi if another wedding is scheduled for the same day as yours. Most locations, as a cour- tesy, will put brides in touch with each other so that decorating plans can be coordinated. It may even be possible for you to collaborate on the selection of flowers and share expenses.

THE RELIGIOUS CEREMONY

Before you finalize your floral designs for the

This birdhouse captures the spirit at a home wedding, preceding page.
Pansies, periwinkle, bachelor buttons, tansy, and trachelium add color to the tiny church
(Alexandra Randall). Flowers are a beautiful welcome: In the winter hang a garland, left, of pine
and boxwood with baby's breath and 'Casablanca' lilies (Alexandra Randall). In the spring,
above, trim a branch with seasonal symbols like this tiny bird's nest surrounded
by lilac, ivy, lilies of the valley, and forsythia (Valorie Hart).

*A baptismal font, above, is perfect to hold rose petals to
shower the newlyweds (Bobby Wiggins). In a simple chapel, vibrant
color will enliven the space—branches of forsythia entwined with mimosa,
American roses, French tulips, ranunculus, and asters, right, create a
luminous golden arch and altar piece (Valorie Hart).*

ceremony, consult the rector or rabbi about your plans. No two churches or temples have the same policy on the use of flowers or other decorations. Most restrictions stem from liability concerns. Some churches ban the use of nylon aisle runners, for example, because they are too slippery. Most churches ask guests not to toss rice or birdseed at the newlyweds after the ceremony. (Both are easy to slip on and birdseed attracts unwanted pigeons.)

Showering the bride and groom with flower petals is prettier and happily has also become the preferred alternative to tossing rice or birdseed. You can arrange for your florist to supply delicate petals from discarded or aging blooms, or they can be gathered from a friend's abundant garden. Most roses and peonies are good sources of petals because of their abundant blooms. Set up a beautiful display of soft, fragrant petals near the exits, so departing guests can help themselves to a handful. Choose either a mixed pastel palette of petals or use only petals that match your color scheme: For an all-white wedding, use all-white petals.

Many churches and synagogues are ornate and require only a little embellishment to create the proper mood for a wedding. Arrangements along every pew or at every altar are wasted; even an arbor at the end of the main aisle can seem too much. The most elaborate interiors look best with a single large design at the altar or twin arrangements on either side of the aisle. Not only is the location best served, but so are your dollars by investing in just one or a few dramatic showpieces rather than numerous small arrangements destined to be lost against the architectural splendor of the space. Spring-blooming branches of forsythia, dogwood, crab-apple, or cherry blossom make captivating arrangements because the size and shape of the branches suit the scale of the space. Long-stemmed flowers are also good choices, such as graceful madonna lilies or calla lilies which would fit perfectly in an all-white design. Avoid short-stemmed or smaller blooms; they become insignificant in a grand environment.

Don't complicate the color scheme. Ultimately, the purity and elegance of simple colors lend far more drama than a rainbow of colors. Always chic, a classic all-white scheme naturally brightens dark, Gothic interiors. Or you can use deep, rich tones to complement the

Gilded birch branches supporting an airy canopy give this huppah a rustic yet delicate quality, left. American roses, Dutch agapanthus, freesias, Queen Anne's lace, 'La Reve' and 'Casablanca' lilies, lilacs, stocks, phlox, sweet william, asparagus ferns, ivy, ruscus, and 'Angélique' tulips decorate the base and candlestands (Valorie Hart, canopy by Angel Threads).

mahogany-hued woods and vivid stained glass of cathedrals. For a fall ceremony, try a mix of branches of red berries, blowsy magenta or blue hydrangeas, and ruby amaryllis; or make a lush palette of deep ruby-edged 'Nicole' and salmon-pink 'Sonia' roses. Alternatively, use branches of fall foliage, like deep red maple or soft yellow crab-apple. For a winter wedding, place evergreen trees at the end of the aisles, and trim the branches with white flowers or gilded pine cones, and use garlands of evergreens to adorn columns or drape pews or altars. Or, use the greenery alone or with clusters of white anemone or gilded holly to punctuate each draping point.

Effective use of color can be particularly striking in a simple church or temple. Bright combinations of flowers create a lively contrast to all-white, pale wood interiors. Yellow is a vibrant choice to enliven simple architecture. Arches of mimosa and wild aster at the end of the aisle capture the freshness of a perfect spring day. Pots of colorful tulips lining the front of the altar or window boxes of sunny ranunculus and wheat grass stand out beautifully against clear glass.

Flowers can serve a practical purpose too: Highlight the family seats with cascades of euphorbia or, if the church or site of the ceremony is large and the guest list small, create a more intimate feeling by using garlands to close off all but the front dozen or so seats needed for guests.

Outside, flowers can trim the front door, gate, and/or lamppost. This not only creates a beautiful welcome for the guests but also serves as a site marker for out-of-towners. A sheaf of wheat for good luck, or, in winter, a wreath of gilded pine cones with a cluster of stephanotis can decorate the front door. Create a fantasy floral topiary using a single branch about two to four inches in diameter and up to six feet high (match the height of the topiary to the scale of the space). Plant the branch in an aged clay pot, top it with a ball of styrofoam, and cover with a variety of hearty blooms such as parrot tulips, azaleas, roses, and phlox. Design a pair of topiaries to stand outside the church or at the head of the aisles inside.

Whatever design options you choose make sure they do not obstruct the ceremony. Pew

*Inside a church or synagogue, baskets generously overflowing with
flowers—Dutch roses, lilac, viburnum, lilies of the valley, phlox, ivy, and
forsythia—can spotlight the family seats, left. For a simpler look, line the aisle with large
pots of daisies, above (both Bobby Wiggins).*

*At an outdoor wedding, hang a swing and cover it with flowers—
creamy yellow-green American roses, narcissus, Dutch asters, viburnum, freesias,
dianthus, and peonies are contrasted by purple trachelium and heather, above. Decorate
architectural elements with flowers—Dutch viburnum, phlox, and dianthus,
right (both Alexandra Randall).*

and aisle decorations must not impede your walk down the aisle, allow plenty of room for your train. The floral decorations should guide the guests' eyes toward the front of the church and not block their vision of the bridal procession or the ceremony.

A traditional Jewish wedding can take place anywhere, as long as the couple is wed under a huppah. This canopied four-leg structure symbolizes shelter and the couple's new home. The word huppah literally means "covering." No religious guidelines dictate the details of the design of the huppah, but it must convey a roof-like appearance.

Imaginative use of flowers and foliage add elegance and color to the traditional huppah. For an enchanted feeling, fashion an awning of smilax vine trimmed with spray roses and full-blown garden roses, and support it on birch-branch legs. Use a mixed palette of roses, concentrating most of the flowers toward the front and side of the huppah, as these are the areas most visible to the guests. Cover the floor under the huppah with moss and let it spread out unevenly beneath it. Finish the design with additional roses at the base of the birch legs to

cover raw edges. For a more classical look, design a formal huppah using fluted white columns as legs and a tulle tent crowned with gilded ivy. Allow the ivy to trail freely around the legs of the huppah to the floor and dot the gilded vine with dozens of stephanotis flowers to create a starry effect.

In churches, altar arrangements are, traditionally, left in place to be enjoyed for the next day of services. Before the wedding, your floral designer will remove any floral debris and will leave the space clean and ready for the ceremony. In any event, the donation fee for the use of the church or synagogue covers the cost of disposal of arrangements after the wedding or whenever the flowers are finally past their prime.

THE HOME CEREMONY

Steeped in pleasant memories, your home offers a sentimental setting for your wedding ceremony. While the image of gracefully descending a staircase into a living room full of admiring family and friends may prove irresistible, before you choose a home ceremony con-

Use flowers to create a pretty wedding site outdoors: In a city yard,
flagstones were temporarily set under an arch, above, entwined with smilax vine,
lilies, gardenias, lilacs, and roses. At its base, a carpet of hyacinths, moss, and grass was
planted; twin urns of crabapple blossoms flank the arch (Zezé).

sider the additional demands it will place on your family. If everyone is comfortable with the idea, prepare yourself for a beautiful, though possibly more hectic, day.

Home weddings require careful planning. You may need to keep your guest list modest so that the crowd can be accommodated. Choose the largest, grandest room for the ceremony; this is usually the living room. If possible, plan to have the wedding performed in front of the fireplace or an expanse of windows: The spot you choose should seem to frame the bridal party. Plan to exchange vows at the far end of the room so there is some length for the procession of the bridal party. To make more space, you may need to move most of the furniture from the room for the day. Store unnecessary pieces in the basement or even in a moving van parked around the corner. Rent ballroom chairs for the guests or arrange the wedding to be a standing-room-only affair.

At home, flowers play an important role in transforming an everyday living room into a special space. Placing potted bulbs, azaleas, or hydrangeas in a row will define an aisle for the bridal procession. If you are using a fireplace as a backdrop, drape the mantel with evergreens and candles for a winter wedding, and prepare the hearth for a fire during the reception. If the room is small, don't light the fire until just before the ceremony—nerves alone will probably make it hot enough for the bride and groom.

Use flowers to create an extravagant and celebratory atmosphere throughout the home. Decorate the front door with a wreath or bouquet of flowers. Or fill large baskets or urns at the entrance with tall flowers, such as delphiniums, hydrangeas, or spring blossoms such as forsythia, dogwood, or magnolia. Your florist can even rent columns—to stand outside the room where the service will take place—and top them with lush arrangements. Adorn railings on the porch or staircase with blossoms and greenery such as smilax or ivy. Since the wedding celebration will naturally spread throughout the house, place arrangements in key locations: hall tables, the landing, side tables in the library or dining room, and don't forget the bathrooms. Any flowers will brighten a room, but if expense is a concern use masses of baby's breath for refreshing, affordable arrangements.

THE OUTDOOR CEREMONY

Imagine the perfect spring or summer day. The light touch of a gentle breeze rippling a lush grassy carpet. A shady spot under a leafy tree blooming with fragrant blossoms. Whether in your own yard or on the capacious grounds of a museum, botanical garden, or park, at the seaside, or on a lakefront, few sites are as appealing as those provided by Mother Nature.

No matter how spectacular or apparently perfect the setting, an outdoor wedding requires practical planning. Although you may have chosen the perfect outdoor site, common sense dictates the need to protect your ceremony against adverse weather with a tent or indoor alternative. For outdoor weddings in summer, avoid the middle of the day when the sun is at its peak.

Like ornate cathedrals, a well-tended garden needs little additional adornment. Pick the most scenic spot for the ceremony and put the natural drama of the landscape to work for you. If there is a natural avenue formed by several trees or garden plants or a "stage" formed by a rise in the ground or a canopy of foliage, plan around it for the ceremony. Avoid areas with overgrown weeds, burnt grass, and flower beds that need pruning. Look for a place under a tree with the broadest canopy of shade, in front of a spectacular fountain, or on a terrace. A plain garden will be brightened by pots of blooming flowers: Narcissus and hyacinths in spring, foxgloves and delphiniums in summer, chrysanthemums in fall.

If a natural spot to use as the wedding site is not convenient, create your own. Your florist can rent trees or blooming plants to define an area for the ceremony, he or she can rent an arch to trim with flowers, or, in spring, fashion an arbor from flowering branches of cherry, crabapple, or dogwood.

Walking to the ceremony re-creates an age-old tradition. Design a long walkway through the garden to the wedding site or to the nearby reception area, using ribbon, draped and knotted from tree to tree, to outline a path. Or overlap long aisle runners end-to-end to construct a path between an avenue of trees for a memorable stroll to the wedding spot.

Choose blooms carefully for garden decorations and bouquets. The sun and heat will wilt most delicate flowers; if possible, all flowers should have a water source. Use water-filled urns or vases to hold arrangements. Bouquets at outdoor ceremonies in summer are best designed with an oasis. Roses, carnations, gladiola, dahlias, chrysanthemums, orchids, and any tropical blooms are more heat-tolerant than most. But lily of the valley, gardenias, pansies, and forget-me-nots are too fragile to withstand hot weather.

For an evening wedding at home give guests a luminous floral welcome with candles like these, on a wreath of heather embellished with lilac and roses. Heather and lilac also cover the wires of the white lights that coil down the columns (Alexandra Randall).

The

Reception

For most newlyweds, the reception is a very special party indeed. Allow plenty of time to plan; you'll need it to develop and organize ideas. Careful planning can make even a simple affair as memorable as the most lavish event.

In ancient cultures, a reception was the legal bond of matrimony. In the early years of the Roman Empire, couples were not officially married until they ate together. During the Middle Ages, the wedding celebration lasted days, even weeks. Plentiful food and

drink symbolized a future blessed with children and financial success. Only towards the end of the Middle Ages did the marriage ceremony become a separate celebration from the wedding feast or reception. To this day, the reception is a lively affair: The ceremony may last only fifteen minutes, but the reception goes on for hours.

CHOOSING A LOCATION

The time to begin searching for the best reception location is right after you become engaged. Often, popular sites must be reserved at least a year in advance. If you don't know where to begin, open the local Yellow Pages and look under party places, country clubs, museums, galleries, marinas, restaurants, and hotels. If you live in a large city, chances are some enterprising soul has put together a list of the best locations, ask at your library. Look in guidebooks if you are considering a country inn. Review travel magazines, city magazines, and articles or special sections of the newspaper for ideas and sources. Special features often cover local party sites. Contact your local newspaper's society editor for more suggestions. But ultimately, the best source for recommendations may be your floral designer, since he or she has probably decorated a reception or party in a variety of places ranging from elegant to simple, grand to small.

If you are planning a large reception, try to engage a floral designer who doubles as a party planner. Some designers specialize in large events and can recommend caterers, musicians, rental services, calligraphers and

Flowers at each place setting, such as these roses backed by gilded rose leaves,
preceding page, add a personal touch that is echoed here by individual sugar-flowered wedding
cakes (Gail Watson). All-white buckets and watering cans brimming with garden flowers are a country
welcome, left. Decorate the porch railing with blooms, above: Separate the flowers from their
stems and tape them to the rail, overlapping to hide the tape and using
water picks for fragile flowers (both Alexandra Randall).

*Whether your reception is held at home or in an unfamiliar location,
flowers add an air of festivity and make a decorated landmark—a lamppost
trimmed with pine and Dutch chrysanthemums, above left, or a gate post decked with a
finial of flowers, above right (both Alexandra Randall).*

*If there is no architectural element to highlight, create welcoming floral
marker: A "parson's" bike with a basket of Dutch gerber daisies, above left, or a
topiary of fresh spring flowers by an open door, above right
(Alexandra Randall; topiary, Blue Meadow).*

whatever else you might need. Others have working relationships with party planners who can handle the party details for you.

Your reception should follow the wedding ceremony as soon as possible. If the reception is not at the same location as the ceremony, allow adequate time for

generous buffet brunch on a restaurant terrace; after a midday service, adjourn to a hotel suite for a simple champagne and cake tea. A late afternoon ceremony could precede cocktails and hors d'oeuvres in the library of a grand estate or country club and a formal sit-down dinner reception.

your guests to travel to the reception location. Plan the time of your ceremony and your reception accordingly. Ideally, the trip between the two locations should take no more than thirty minutes. Be sure to allow for delays caused by road construction, rush hour, or shopping traffic. Provide guests with maps if the reception is in an unusual location.

The time of day should influence the type of reception you choose to have. You might follow a morning service at a chapel with a

The mood and color palette of the decorations should serve to unify the ceremony and reception to keep the atmosphere flowing. The atmosphere initiated at the ceremony should extend to all details of the reception without mixing moods. Even the attire of the wedding party should blend harmoniously with the overall design. For a wedding in a Gothic cathedral followed by a reception in a gracious old-world manor house, for example, wear a classic bridal gown. In a tra-

Sleek calla lilies are easily gilded with gold spray paint. Because
of their dramatic shape they can be used sparingly and still make a stunning
arrangement, left (Curtis M. Godwin). Cherubs are a universal symbol of romance. For
a charming entryway or window, use them to fashion decorative tiebacks for
drapes and trim with blossoms, above (Valorie Hart).

ditional setting, you wouldn't choose to be married in a modern mini-dress suited to a cosmopolitan locale, nor select eyelet tablecloths and baskets overflowing with grasses and wildflowers, which would look best in an outdoor, country location.

DECORATING THE RECEPTION

Once you choose a location, review it with your floral designer. Let the architecture guide your decorating. Not every surface has to be, or in larger locations can be, decorated with flowers. Instead, take advantage of central locations and any existing dramatic design features like staircases, columns, mantels, and archways and make them focal points for floral arrangements and trimmings. Hang garlands of boxwood, evergreens, or ivy across mantels, over doorways, down col-

umns. Place arrangements of lilies, long stemmed roses, or hydrangeas in hearths, over mantles, on center and hall tables, at entrances. Follow the scale of each location: The height and width of each arrangement should be influenced by the proportions of the surrounding space. One fabulous design in each room makes a more impressive statement than a number of insignificant bowls of flowers scattered everywhere.

If you have a little imagination and are resourceful you can manipulate any space. Of course, it's much easier to meet your expectations if the location requires only minor embellishments. A "no frills" location is not always the most economical choice: Ultimately, it may be less expensive to rent a more interesting space than to completely transform a plain room into a rich environment. However, almost any number of ornamental

Arrangements can be striking and affordable too. Use petite versions of the flowers for the bridal table for each guest table, left (Valorie Hart). Or, try a beautiful, inexpensive and easy to execute design, like these gilded clay pots and miniature roses, above, for a candlelight ceremony (Carolien Stikker).

Sometimes one stunning arrangement is all you really need. A cachepot
brimming with flowers—lilac, 'Little silver' roses, Dutch 'gooseneck' veronica,
trachelium, artemesia, and English lavender—makes a gift table into a focal point, above
(Alexandra Randall). A heart-shaped wreath of American roses is a romantic
alternative to a mantelpiece arrangement, right (Carolien Stikker).

With their porcelain-like delicacy, pastillage flowers make a wedding cake even more beautiful, top (Sylvia Weinstock). A heart-shaped basket packed with tiny blooms on each table looks good enough to eat but is just for show, bottom (Lawrence Becker). Serve individual cakes decorated with the flowers from your bouquet, right (Gail Watson).

accessories can be rented, including works of art, sculpture, decorative screens, mirrors, even ornate birdcages.

Use lighting to establish a mood. Raise or lower chandeliers to soften or intensify the light. Replace or remove light bulbs to lower the wattage, or create a truly romantic atmosphere with candlelight. Place leafy plants in front of windows to soften the daylight. Tiny white lights can be woven through trees for a starry evening wedding.

Trees and potted plants are a natural complement to cut flowers when decorating any space, and sometimes by virtue of their scale they may have more impact. Your florist can rent them from nurseries. The best tree to use depends upon the season. Ficus trees, palms, topiaries, and evergreens are almost always available and they can be placed throughout the reception site. Use them to flank doorways, delineate an outdoor reception area, or frame the bar or buffet table. Stand trees in attractive clay or porcelain planters, and cover the dirt with moss or cut flowers to finish the look. Scatter stones at the base of aged clay pots to evoke an outdoor feeling. In central locations, tall evergreen trees trimmed with pastel azalea blooms lend a festive air to holiday weddings. Put dwarf azaleas, potted hydrangeas, or topiaries on bars and tables.

Nurseries are also great sources for flowering plants, baskets overflowing with fuchsias, impatiens, or geraniums. Hang them on front porches, set them on top of columns allowing the vines or blooms to cascade down, or suspend them under tents at each support pole. Place flowering plants in beautiful pots; set four to five in a row to create a bandstand backdrop, to highlight a stairway or the entrance to a tent, or to block off an unwanted exit.

Party-rental companies can provide everything you need from tents to tables and chairs, linens, china, and stemware. You and your florist can add your own personal touches based on your design scheme. For an imaginative and useful showpiece, rent a beautiful birdcage and fill it with flowers or lovebirds, then set it on a large table at an entryway with the place cards.

Tables naturally call for flowers. Center-

*Flowers are natural art: Here a gilded frame holds a living tableau in
the jewel-like tones of roses, hydrangeas, orchids, narcissus, and Dutch 'gloriosa'
lilies, above (Preston Bailey). To give the bride's chair a special look, right, entwine it with
smilax vine and ivy and trim it with roses, white lilacs, and ruffled
ribbon rosettes (Valorie Hart).*

pieces can be as simple or elaborate as you wish. Trim candelabra with blossoms by nestling small blooms such as miniature white roses at the base of each candle. Put individual bud vases each holding a single poppy at every place setting. For napkin rings, use gilded ivy brightened with a sprig of stephanotis.

Flowers can even add a fresh touch to place cards: glue a fresh Serena rose to each card, or have an illustrator paint flowers on them individually. No matter what the table decor, make sure the centerpieces do not obstruct the view and conversation of the guests.

To decorate buffet tables and trays with flowers, consider the amount of space needed for food and design the arrangement accordingly. For a table with finger foods, fashion a cornucopia of fruits, nuts, and flowers to spill across the table. Or rest a narrow window box along the back of the table, filled with an array of seasonal blooms or all-yellow daffodils for a splash of fresh color. Platters of appetizers and drinks circulated by waiters

can be trimmed with flowers such as a single open lily, with its staining pollen buds removed, anchored at its base to the tray with a touch of florist putty.

The bride's table demands a distinctive floral decor. If a long table is used, the arrangement should be kept low so all guests have a clear view of the bridal party. A garland works best. For an elegant spring look, drape a garland of peonies, phlox, stock, and euphorbia from corner to corner. Gild eucalyptus or bay leaves for a dramatic holiday garland and trim the corners of the table with pine cones or white 'Casablanca' lilies. Weave three-inch-wide pink and white satin ribbons for a unique tablecloth. Scatter petals on the guest tables to pick up the color scheme. Or, use white or pastel tulle over a basic white cloth, and top off the table with a bowl of sweet-peas. For a charming country scene, use gingham tablecloths with a basket of daisies as the centerpiece.

The wedding cake is a sumptuous treat and

a focal point at any reception. Trim this confection with a cascade of candy flowers or surround the cake plate with real blooms. Fresh flowers can also decorate the layers of the cake. Flowers on the cake should be washed thoroughly and should not be eaten— chances are that they have been treated at some time with pesticides.

Because it is a classic location for bridal photos, it's important to showcase the cake. Use ribbons to suspend a wreath of boxwood mixed with pastel blooms—stock, freesia, dianthus, and alstromeria—above. Or, cover the table with white linen and top it with an assortment of pressed flowers: Pansies, daffodils and hydrangeas are easy to press in advance and place under a glass top.

OUTDOOR RECEPTIONS

Outdoor reception areas can be manipulated as easily as indoor sites. Unless you are a dyed-in-the-wool gambler, it's wise to set up tents or have them available in case of bad weather. Tents not only provide protection from rain or chill, they offer important shaded areas on sunny days.

If you choose not to use a tent, plan your reception around naturally shady locations. Select the most beautiful shade tree, and cut plywood or rent a special table to encircle it. Use this cool spot for a buffet table. Scatter guest tables around this area, with market umbrellas placed over each table. Trim the edges of the umbrellas with heather and asters and wind an additional garland down each center pole, letting it trail onto the table. For hot days, lay a keepsake fan trimmed with sprigs of fragrant jasmine at every place setting.

For a poolside wedding, stand potted palm trees at the corners of the pool and float large blooms like hibiscus in the water. In the evening, float candles in the pool for a romantic look, and plant citronella torches around the circumference.

Traditionally the wedding guest is sent home with a keepsake—
a token by which to remember the special day. If you plan a warm
weather ceremony, leave a fan with a knot of fragrant herbs at every seat, left—
practical, beautiful, sentimental. The most romantic receptions are lit with candlelight
—don't forget to add a few flowers to enhance the mood, above
(both Alexandra Randall).

The Bridal

Trousseau

Although photographs and videos capture the treasured details of the day, your wedding flowers can be preserved as a floral trousseau evoking memories in ways celluloid never can. Unfortunately, the bridal bouquet is usually tossed to a cluster of friends at the end of the reception; the lucky one who catches it, so tradition has it, will become the next bride. If your bouquet is too beautiful to throw away, have your floral designer make two, one to toss and one to keep for yourself. In fact, if

you know you want to preserve your bouquet, ask the designer to deliver a duplicate after you return from your honeymoon.

The following pages offer ideas for mementos you can make yourself or have a professional create from your wedding bouquet. If you decide to preserve your bouquet yourself, practice on other flowers first. Preservation works best when your bouquet is still fresh. Ask your mother or maid of honor to refrigerate your flowers immediately after the ceremony until you are ready to preserve them.

DRYING FLOWERS

Air-drying your bouquet is simple. For best results, remove all foliage and retie the flowers with a cotton string at the end of the stems. Securely tie a large brown paper bag over the flowers and hang them upside down in a dry closet. Protect the bag from jostling. The flowers should be dry in two to three weeks. Most sturdy flowers— statice, lavender, hydrangeas, roses, strawflowers, baby's breath—dry well with this technique.

Bouquets can also be preserved intact by freeze-drying, a service offered by many dried-flower shops. The quick drying crystallizes the blooms, which become fragile but almost lifelike. Any flower can be dried using this method.

Dried flowers from your bouquet can add delicate decorative touches throughout the home. Trim a mirrored frame with dried blossoms for your bedroom dresser. Decorate the

An unusual holiday nosegay of gilded poppy and lotus pods, pinecones, pecans and chestnuts, fresh and dried seeded eucalyptus, and dried nigella, preceding page, is a bouquet to keep forever (Blue Meadow Flowers). To air-dry your bouquet, tie it with raffia or cotton and hang it upside down, left—hydrangeas, peonies, mimosa, artemesia, zinnias, and sage work well (VSF). Or press your bridal blossoms, above, and re-create your bouquet to frame (Anne Plowden).

A photograph from your wedding day, top, will be even more special if
its frame is decorated with dried flowers from your bouquet (Flowers Forever).
Personalize your wedding album, bottom, with ribbons and pressed flowers from your
bouquet (Alexandra Randall).

edge of a basket, fill it with aromatic pot-pourri, and place it on a hall table. Create a collage of dried flowers, or a replica of your bouquet to frame.

Flowers can also be dried with a desicant to maintain their natural color and shape. Flowers with soft petals, such as peonies, anemones, and daffodils dry well this way. You can use silica gel, which is available in craft shops, following the instructions on the label, or use borax, available in pharmacies, mixed one part to three parts cornmeal. Sift one inch of the borax mixture into a large box. Use very fresh, turgid, dew-free blooms—drops of water will cause spots—trim the stems to an inch below the buds. (Stems generally do not dry well and are not necessary for these projects.) Nestle the flowers gently into the mixture and fill cup-shaped blooms with it, making sure they don't touch each other. Flowers with a single row of petals, like daisies, should be placed bloom side down on a small mound of borax mix to preserve their shapes. Multi-petaled blooms, like roses, can be dried upright; blooms on stalks, such as delphiniums, should lie sideways in the mix. Place about two inches of the borax mixture over the flowers. Cover the box and let it rest two to ten days, until the flowers are paper dry. Gently shake off the borax mixture, then use a soft bristled paint-brush to carefully dust off any remaining particles. For a romantic first-month anniversary present to your husband, glue the buds to a frame and insert a picture from your wedding.

PRESSING FLOWERS

Pressing flowers is an age-old preservation technique. It is easy to do and the results can be used in many ways. You can re-create your bouquet and frame it; decorate thank-you cards with a blossom from your bouquet; fill a scrap book with floral mementos of your wedding; or, instead of a photo or in addition to one, place a pressed flower in a locket engraved with your wedding date.

Single, flat flowers with one layer of petals are easiest to press. Using sharp scissors remove the stem as close to the base of the fresh, dew-free flower as possible. Any flowers, such as roses or ranunculus, that have multiple levels of petals should be picked apart and the petals pressed separately. Composite blooms like hydrangea should be broken into tiny florets and pressed individually. After the pressing is complete, the flower can be reassembled or the petals or florets used in a scattered design. Small blossoms like pansies and violets can be pressed whole. A daffodil can be sliced in half. Small buds such as baby's breath can be pressed sideways: Use the tip of your finger to gently press the bud onto the paper and leave a short stem for a better look.

When pressing flowers try to handle the flowers as little as possible. Place them on white untextured blotting paper (available at stationery stores) and make sure they do not touch each other. Cover the flowers with another sheet of blotting paper. Then sandwich the paper between two pieces of stiff cardboard. Either use a flower press or cover the cardboard with large, heavy books and leave undisturbed for five to six weeks in a warm, dry room. Resist the temptation to check on the blooms: A longer drying process ensures a better retention of color. Once dry, handle the blooms carefully; use tweezers to lift the pressed flowers.

Alternatively, you can make your bouquet into a fragrant potpourri. Remove petals from the flowers and scatter them in a flat basket or on a screen; cover the petals with cheesecloth to protect them from dust. Let them sit open on a shelf until dry. In a large bowl, add a bit of a favorite herb such as lavender or lemon balm for better fragrance and mix gently. If you prefer a headier scent, add a drop or two of essence or oil, available at bath shops. Place the mixture in a sealed glass container to mature the scent and shake it occasionally to blend the aroma. Keep the potpourri in a jar, perhaps the empty perfume bottle from your wedding day, or make a sachet from a square of tulle tied with a ribbon from your bouquet and keep it in your lingerie drawer.

If your bouquet included fragrant flowers such as hyacinths, jasmine or freesias, you can distill a fragrant bath oil from the blooms. Pack a small jar full of blossoms and fill it with warm, extra-light almond, avocado, or olive oil. Cover it and leave it in a sunny place for one month. Shake the jar occasionally to mix the contents. Tie a swatch of cheesecloth over the mouth of the jar to strain out the blossoms with a ribbon from your bouquet. Use the prepared oil for baths or massages.

You don't have to use real flowers to capture the beauty of your bouquet forever. Commission an illustrator to paint a portrait of your bouquet or to decorate one of your wedding invitations with flowers used in your bouquet. Frame it as a beautiful gift to yourself that you'll treasure always.

Finally, to keep your actual bouquet forever, carry a dried or silk arrangement on your wedding day. You'll always have the exact bouquet to enjoy. Place the flowers in a vase at home to keep the memory of your wedding day always close. Or save the bouquet in a box packed with tissue. Take it out in a reaffirmation ceremony on your tenth, twenty-fifth, or golden wedding anniversary, and say "I do" all over again.

*A dried bouquet like this of wheat, oats, and roses, above,
is a lasting memento that will always evoke precious wedding memories. Keep it
carefully boxed with tissue and use it on anniversaries as a centerpiece
to treasure (Flowers Forever).*

Resources and Acknowledgments

CREDITS

See Resources to contact any of the following suppliers:

Half title: Pamphlet, Kate's Paperie. **Title verso:** Dress, Carolina Herrera Couture Bridal Collection; earrings, Cultured Pearl Association of America; gloves, Fownes Bros.; hair/makeup, Timmothy Montgomery; location, Wako Hardy-Sasaki Studio. **Page 6:** Cachepot, Wolfman-Gold & Good Co.; ribbon, Vaban. **Page 8:** Petticoat and bustier, Vera Wang for Vera Wang Bridal House, Ltd.; location, Vera Wang Bridal House. **Page 9:** Ribbon, Vaban. **Page 10:** Headpiece, La Sposa Veils; earrings, York & Essex Designs for D.P. Accessories; hair/makeup, Patricia Bowden. **Page 11:** Dress, Christian Dior Bridals; necklace, Cultured Pearl Association of America; gloves, La Crasia; hair/makeup, Timmothy Montgomery; location, Wako Hardy-Sasaki Studio. **Page 12:** Calligraphy, Bernard Maisner; card illustration, Amy L. Thornton; music stand, Dampierre & Co.; backdrop, Wendy Umanoff Painted Surfaces. **Page 13:** Location, White and Gold Suite at The Plaza Hotel. **Page 14:** Calligraphy, Pendragon, Ink.; ribbons, Offray; fabric, La Sposa Veils. **Page 15:** Luggage, Gucci; location, The Plaza Hotel. **Page 16:** Slipcover, Siskin-Valls. **Page 18:** Slipcover, Siskin-Valls; location, White and Gold Suite at The Plaza Hotel. **Page 20:** Chair and screen, ABC Carpet & Home; shoes, Peter Fox; tulle, La Sposa Veils. **Page 21:** Blouse and vest, Norma Kamali; skirt, Ann Lawrence; earrings, Kenneth Jay Lane; hair/makeup, Patricia Bowden. **Page 23:** Bench and screen, Dampierre & Co.; ribbon, Vaban. **Page 24, top:** Fichu, Cross & Spellen; chair, Dampierre & Co.; **bottom:** Tissue papers and ribbon, Kate's Paperie; chair, ABC Carpet & Home. **Page 25, top:** Gloves, La Crasia; **bottom:** Table, Dampierre & Co.; ribbon, Vaban. **Page 28:** Coat rack, Zona. **Page 29:** Dress, Norma Kamali; gloves, La Crasia; earrings, Kenneth Jay Lane; hair/makeup, Timmothy Montgomery. **Page 30:** Dress, Norma Kamali; veil, La Sposa Veils; hair/makeup, Timmothy Montgomery. **Page 31:** Dress, Lynda Joy; basket, Shabby Chic; gloves, Fownes Bros. **Page 32:** Ottoman, ABC Carpet & Home; tulle, La Sposa Veils; ribbon, Vaban. **Page 33:** Ribbon, Vaban; platter, Cheryl Henry at Henry & Sagalyn. **Page 34:** Posy holder, mirrored tray, and heart pillboxes, Treasures from the Past/Antiques by Dorene. **Page 35:** Dress, Ann Lawrence Antiques; earrings and pin, Treasures from the Past/Antiques by Dorene; hair, Patricia Bowden; makeup, Timmothy Montgomery. **Page 36:** Petticoat, Claudia Bruce; tulle veil, La Sposa Veils; hair/makeup, Patricia Bowden. **Page 38:** Dress, Lynda Joy; earrings, Kenneth Jay Lane; hair/makeup, Patricia Bowden. **Page 40:** Shoes, Dyeables. **Page 42:** Hat and hat boxes, Quina Fonseca Design Studio; bench, Dampierre & Co. **Page 43:** Bridal gown, Christian Dior available at Vera Wang Bridal House, Ltd.; gloves, La Crasia; earrings, Kenneth Jay Lane; hat, Tia Mazza; hair/makeup, Patricia Bowden. **Page 44:** Dinner jacket, After Six. **Page 45:** Pique vest, After Six; scarf and bow tie, available through David Glazer; cufflinks, Mish; top hat, Worth & Worth. **Page 46:** Wedding bands, Mish; pocket watch, Treasures from the Past/Antiques by Dorene; bow tie, available through David Glazer; leather jewelry box, Kate's Paperie. **Page 48, left & right:** dresses, Susan Sullivan Designs for Fine Choices; grooming for both, Patricia Bowden; watering can, Lexington Gardens. **Page 49, left:** Dress, Ann Lawrence Antiques; **right:** Dress, Christian Dior Bridals; grooming for both, Patricia Bowden. **Page 50:** Hat, Tia Mazza; sunglasses, James Arpad; crystal posy, Ruth Silverman for Lynda Joy; silk flower handbag, Dulken & Derrick; earrings, James Arpad; gloves, Diane Paxton. **Page 51:** Tablecloth, White Linen. **Page 52:** Birdhouse, Wolfman-Gold & Good Co.; calligraphy and card, Pendragon, Ink. **Page 54:** Location, Carolina Church of Brookhaven, Setauket, NY. **Page 56:** Cherub birdbath, Henfeathers available at Special Effects. **Page 58:** Table, linen, and glassware, Party Rental, Ltd. **Page 60:** Basket, Ouzts & Company available at The Garden Shop at M & A. **Page 61:** Aged clay pots, Lexington Gardens; tulle ribbon, Offray. **Page 64:** Ballroom chairs, Party Rental, Ltd. **Page 68:** China, flatware, Party Rental Ltd.; table cloth, Holly Lueders for Caryatid Collection. **Page 70:** Watering cans and buckets, Wolfman-Gold & Good Co; chair, Special Effects. **Page 71:** Cherub, Vintage Verandah, available at Marders Garden Shop and Nursery. **Page 73, left:** Basket, Palachek available at The Baywoods; hat, Tia Mazza; ribbon, Wolfman-Gold & Good Co. **Page 74:** Vase, Zona; calligraphy, Pendragon, Ink.; location, White and Gold Suite at The Plaza Hotel. **Page 76:** Chairs, tables, linens, china, glassware, and flatware, Party Rental Ltd.; chandelier, Lexington Gardens; location, Grand Ballroom, The Puck Building. **Page 77:** Candle stands, Wolfman-Gold & Good Co.; ribbon, Vaban. **Page 78:** Handpainted tole, Henry & Sagalyn; gift boxes, Tiffany & Co. **Page 79:** Ribbon, Vaban. **Page 80, top:** Cake server, Stephen Dweck available at Bergdorf Goodman; location, White and Gold Suite at The Plaza Hotel. **Page 81:** Cake plate, William-Wayne & Co. **Page 82:** American period gilded frame, Eli Wilner & Co.; china and flatware, Party Rental, Ltd.; linens, Angel Threads. **Page 83:** Chair and china, Party Rental, Ltd.; tablecloth, Angel Threads; vase, Dish-Ta-Henge distributed through Showroom Seven. **Page 84:** Fan and calligraphy, Heather Belle, Ink for Alexandra Randall Flowers; parasol, Ann Lawrence Antiques; chair, Special Effects. **Page 85:** Candlesticks,

Wolfman-Gold & Good Co. **Page 90:** Wedding photographer, Rob Fraser. **Page 90:** Scrapbook, Kate's Paperie; wedding photographer, Rob Fraser. **Page 93:** Bridal veil, Belle Meline. **Back jacket (clockwise from top left):** Location, Vera Wang Bridal House. Aged clay pots, Lexington Gardens; tulle ribbon, Offray. China, stemware, flatware, and linens, Party Rental, Ltd.; candleabra, Dampierre & Co. Dresses, Ann Lawrence Antiques; grooming, Patricia Bowden; linens, White Linen.

RESOURCES
Floral Designers

Work by the following designers appears in this book. They are experienced in all kinds of weddings and special events. Those with an asterisk have retail shops; others, the private designers, can be contacted directly for appointments or to order flowers.

Preston Bailey
(212) 683-0035

L. Becker Flowers*
Lawrence Becker
(212) 439-6001

Blue Meadow Flowers*
Michael Mitrano
Tom Tellas
(212) 979-8618

Flowers Forever*
Debra Felberbaum
(212) 308-0088

Curtis M. Godwin, Flowers
(212) 645-2639

Valorie Hart Designs
(212) 633-0260

Leslie Kyle Ferrar Designs
(717) 437-2446

Alexandra Randall
(516) 862-9291

Tutti Fiori
Carolien Stikker
(718) 852-4458

VSF*
Jack Follmer
Spruce Roden
(212) 206-7236

Bobby Wiggins
(212) 627-1412

Zezé*
(212) 753-7767

Preserved and Artificial Flowers

Dulken & Derrick
(212) 929-3614
Hand-crafted silk flowers

Ruth Silverman for Lynda Joy, Inc.
(212) 627-2335
Hand-crafted, all-beaded flowers to order

Ann Plowden, Inc.
(617) 267-4705
Pressing and framing of wedding bouquets

Floral Organizations

Flower Council of Holland
(212) 307-1818
Consumer information

Frank W. Manker
(516) 289-5294
American grown roses; wholesale only

Roses, Inc.
(517) 339-9544
Consumer information

Bridal Gowns, Gifts, Wedding Services, and Accessories

Retail stores are highlighted with an asterisk; they will usually provide a bridal registry. Contact custom services for appointments or information. Private suppliers will work directly with you. Wholesalers and manufacturers will guide you to the nearest store that carries their merchandise.

ABC Carpet & Home*
(212) 473-3000
Antiques, furniture, decorative accessories

After Six
(800) 423-8376
Men's formal wear

Angel Threads
(212) 673-4592
Custom linens, wedding canopies

James Arpad
(212) 944-9406
Austrian crystal accessories

The Baywoods*
(516) 726-5950
Decorative floral accessories

Heather Belle, Ink
(804) 286-2940
Hand-lettered wedding invitations

Belle Meline
(516) 473-1039
Custom bridal veils

Patricia Bowden
(718) 832-0682
Hair and makeup stylist

Claudia Bruce
(212) 685-2810
Custom clothing

Cross & Spellen*
(212) 675-4862
Clothing, accessories

Cultured Pearl Assoc. of America
(212) 688-5580
Consumer information

Dampierre & Co.*
(212) 966-5474
Antiques, decorative accessories

Christian Dior Bridals
(215) 659-8700
Bridal gowns

Dyeables, Inc.
(800) 431-2000
in New York: (914) 878-8000
Dyeable shoes, handbags

Fine Choices
(414) 964-1756
Children's clothing

Quina Fonseca Design Studio
(212) 353-1765
Custom millinery

Peter Fox Shoes*
(212) 431-7426
Bridal shoe salon

Rob Fraser Photography
(212) 677-4589
Candid and formal photographs

The Garden Shop at M & A*
(516) 676-0980
Decorative accessories

David Glazer
(212) 582-0042
Men's accessories

Gucci*
Over 30 stores nationwide
Fashions, accessories

Anne-Stuart Hamilton
(212) 924-8695
Party planner, gift design

Henry & Sagalyn
(212) 289-3094
Hand-painted cachepots

Carolina Herrera Couture
(212) 575-0557
Bridal gowns

Lynda Joy, Inc.
(212) 627-2335
Couture bridal gowns

OMO Norma Kamali*
(212) 957-9797
Bridal department

Kate's Paperie*
(212) 633-0570
Handmade papers, gifts

La Crasia Gloves
(212) 447-1043
Bridal gloves

La Sposa Veil*
(212) 354-4729
Bridal fabrics, custom veils

Kenneth Jay Lane*
(212) 751-6166
Costume jewelry

Ann Lawrence Antiques
(212) 302-4036
Bridal gowns, accessories, furniture

Holly Lueders
(212) 246-8150
Home design collection

Lexington Gardens*
(212) 861-4390
Decorative floral accessories

Bernard Maisner Calligraphy Studio
(212) 477-6776
Hand lettering by appointment

Marders Garden Shop and Nursery*
(516) 537-3700
Decorative floral accessories

Tia Mazza
(212) 629-9438
Millinery

Mish
(212) 535-7450
Jewelry

Party Rental Ltd.
(212) 594-8510
Chairs, tables, linens, china etc.

Diane Paxton
(617) 666-0807
Custom bridal accessories

Pendragon, Ink.
(508) 234-6843
Custom wedding invitations, menus, stationery

C. M. Offray & Son, Inc.
(908) 879-4700
Ribbons

Shabby Chic*
(213) 394-1975
(212) 274-9842
Furniture, accessories

Siskin-Valls, Inc.
(212) 752-3790
Custom interior design

Special Effects*
(516) 928-7913
Decorative accessories

Amy L. Thornton
(212) 316-2677
Hand lettering, illustration

Tiffany & Co.*
(800) 526-0649
Jewelry, gifts, invitations

Treasures from the Past/ Antiques by Dorene
(212) 818-9078
Vintage jewelry, accessories

Vaban Ribbons
(212) 889-3088

Vera Wang Bridal House, Ltd.*
(212) 879-1700
Full service bridal salon

Wako Hardy-Sasaki Studio
(212) 533-0004
Antiques, photo-studio

Gail Watson Custom Cakes
(212) 982-3345
Custom cakes

Sylvia Weinstock Cakes
(212) 925-6698
Custom cakes

White Linen, Inc.
(518) 732-4410
Linens

William-Wayne & Co.*
(212) 477-3182
Decorative accessories

Eli Wilner & Co.*
(212) 744-6521
Period frames, mirrors.

Wolfman-Gold & Good Co.*
(212) 431-1888
All-white decorative accessories

Worth & Worth
(800) 428-7467
Men's hats

York & Essex Designs
(212) 966-6919
Jewelry, accessories

Zona*
(212) 925-6750
American decorative accessories

Locations

The Plaza Hotel
(212) 546-5485
Lawrence Harvey, Executive Director of Catering
Full service hotel. Suites and ballrooms available for weddings and special events. Brochure available.

The Puck Building
(212) 274-8900
Stephanie Rose, Director
Turn-of-the-century landmark building. Ballrooms accommodate 50–1,000 people. Brochure available.

ACKNOWLEDGMENTS

Special thanks to some very important people who assisted in the creation of this book: My tireless assistant stylist, Cindy Zdzienicki; my intrepid researcher, Russell McBride; the accommodating people at two tremendous flower organizations Niek Van Rest and Bob Perilla of the Flower Council of Holland and Heather Kelly and Bill Mankers of American Rose Growers; the generous Florence de Dampierre, Kay Towne, and Pauline Kelly; the talented Patricia Bowden and Timmothy Montgomery; all my helpful co-editors at *Bride's*, especially Denise O'Donoghue, Rachel Leonard, Susan Keller, Donna Ferrari, Milli Martini, Debi Jason, Elizabeth Rundlett, and Rene Sheffey; and, of course, the very talented, energetic floral designers whose beautiful work is featured in this book.